Oladipo Agboluaje

IMMUNE

T0314858

OBERON BOOKS
LONDON

WWW.OBERONBOOKS.COM

First published in 2015 by Oberon Books Ltd
521 Caledonian Road, London N7 9RH
Tel: +44 (0) 20 7607 3637 / Fax: +44 (0) 20 7607 3629
e-mail: info@oberonbooks.com
www.oberonbooks.com

A catalogue record for this book is available from the British
Library.

PB ISBN: 9781783199419
E ISBN: 9781783199426

Cover design by James Illman

Visit www.oberonbooks.com to read more about all our books
and to buy them. You will also find features, author interviews and
news of any author events, and you can sign up for e-newsletters
so that you're always first to hear about our new releases.

IMMUNE
BY OLADIPO AGBOLUAJE

ROYAL & DERNGATE NORTHAMPTON

CAST AND CREATIVES

ALBERT **JAKUB MADEJ**	DIRECTOR **CHRISTOPHER ELMER-GORRY**
ANGIE **EMILY WINNETT**	DESIGNER
BELLA **ESME JOY ALLEN**	**CARL DAVIES**
BONNIE **BETHANY PRIDDY**	LIGHTING AND PROJECTION DESIGNER
CRAIG **OWEN HOWARD**	**DAVID MIDDLETON**
DENISE **SCARLETT JORDAN**	SOUND DESIGN
ERIC **JARZINHO RAPOZ**	**MARTIN THOMPSON**
FELICITY **ELLA GODFREY**	ASSISTANT DIRECTOR **SUBIKA ANWAR**
GEORGE **JAKE CARTER**	STAGE MANAGER
JANE **CARLA KENNEDY**	**MADELEINE WILLIS**
NICHOLAS **HAL GALLAGHER**	ASSISTANT PRACTITIONER/ASM **AMY COLLINGWOOD**
PENNY **JODI TWINER**	
PETER **ETHAN KELLY**	For Royal & Derngate Youth Theatre and Young Company
SAMSON **LUKE NUNN**	YOUTH THEATRE ASSOCIATE **ASHLEY ELBOURNE**

YOUNG COMPANY PARTICIPANT
EMILIE WAYMONT

First Performance:

ALL OTHER PARTS ARE PLAYED BY
MEMBERS OF THE COMPANY

Royal & Derngate Young Company
Thursday 2 July 2015

A NOTE FROM THE DIRECTOR CHRISTOPHER ELMER-GORRY

Working with Royal and Derngate Young Company on the creation of a new play for the Royal auditorium has been a really exciting process. Beginning in September 2014, participants from all three of the co-commissioning partners worked with Oladipo to create a brand-new play.

Our process began with workshops in all venues, exploring a variety of themes from religion to technology. Over the course of the next few months, each Youth Theatre/Young Company developed their ideas in consultation with Dipo. The discoveries from the initial workshops were then shaped to create a first draft.

It was a pleasure to host the Research & Development weekend at Royal & Derngate in January 2015 where we welcomed young people from both Theatre Royal Plymouth and West Yorkshire Playhouse. The weekend was spent exploring the use of direct address/dialogue, as well as character and narrative. Over the weekend, I worked closely with Dipo to communicate the needs of the different groups, in addition to workshopping elements of the script that we wanted to develop further. It was a really useful part of the process for the young people as it enabled them to get a clear insight into the process of creating a brand-new play.

For me, one of the most exciting elements of the script is its inherent theatricality. The challenge for our actors in Northampton has been the mixture of direct address and dialogue, along with characters' internal thoughts against physical action. These challenges led onto our own discussions as a company regarding the Theatrical Rules for our production. The challenge of these different storytelling techniques has required us to consider that the audience doesn't necessarily need to see everything we are told…but we do need to be consistent with the way we tell our story. Adopting a heightened theatrical world, inspired by the world of the graphic novel, allows us to push our audience's imagination; a much more exciting starting point than if we were to show everything literally.

For the premiere in Northampton, Carl Davies created a beautiful design which allowed us to shift locations quickly and easily. We discussed the possibility of physically framing the space, playing with light and dark, and encouraging shadows. It was also important for us to create a playground for our actors where we could develop the design requirements as the rehearsals progressed. For both of us, the aesthetic world of our production would be something that was simplistic enough to change location, visually stunning enough to keep our audience engaged and, most importantly, represent a theatrical world that feels like a series of stills from a graphic novel.

It has been really refreshing to work on a piece of work for young performers that allowed us to be so theatrical. We are often faced with naturalistic representations of a young person's life or experience and Immune enabled us to explore the traditional elements of naturalism whilst at the same time utilising the theatrical possibilities of a dystopian world.

ROYAL DERNGATE & NORTHAMPTON

Chief Executive **Martin Sutherland**

Artistic Director **James Dacre**

Royal & Derngate, Northampton, is the main venue for arts and entertainment in Northamptonshire. Last year more than 290,000 people saw shows and films at Royal & Derngate and another 22,000 saw co-produced work across the country.

Recent years have seen the increased profile of Royal & Derngate as one of the major producing venues in the country, including being named Regional Theatre of the Year by the inaugural Stage 100 Awards in 2011.

The 2015 *Made In Northampton* season includes world premieres of Arthur Miller's *The Hook*, and Aldous Huxley's *Brave New World* in an adaptation by Dawn King, with music composed by These New Puritans.

The 2014 *Made In Northampton* season included premieres of Mike Poulton's adaptation of *A Tale of Two Cities*, with music composed by Rachel Portman, Tamsin Oglesby's adaptation of Feydeau's *Every Last Trick*, Dan O'Brien's *The Body of An American* in a co-production with the Gate Theatre, London, Nicholas Wright's adaptation of Pat Barker's *Regeneration*, and, building on Royal & Derngate's national reputation for innovative work for children and young people, Ella Hickson's *Merlin* and Phil Porter's *Moominsummer Madness* in a co-production with Polka Theatre.

Other recent highlights have included *Cat on a Hot Tin Roof* with original music by White Lies, *A Midsummer Night's Dream*, the world premiere of Ayub Khan Din's adaptation of *To Sir, With Love*, and the 50th Anniversary production of Alan Ayckbourn's *Mr Whatnot*. Festival Of Chaos featured as part of London 2012 Festival and included premieres of three adaptations of classic plays – *The Bacchae*, *Blood Wedding* and *Hedda Gabler*; *Spring Storm* and *Beyond The Horizon* transferred to the National Theatre, and four-time Olivier Award-nominated *End Of The Rainbow* (co-produced with Lee Dean) transferred to the West End and Broadway.

The venue also presents a diverse range of visiting work on both the Derngate and Royal Stages, including musicals, dance, comedy and music, and the wide-ranging *Get Involved* programme engages with schools, families and communities in Northamptonshire and beyond, with over 21,000 participants last year.

Royal & Derngate also continues to work in partnership to manage The Core at Corby Cube and in 2013 opened an onsite 88-seat cinema adjacent to Derngate auditorium, named after one of the theatre's most famous alumni, the Errol Flynn Filmhouse.

IMMUNE
By Oladipo Agboluaje

CAST AND CREATIVES

GEORGE **EDDIE BRECKENRIDGE**
CAT **ROSEMARY CLOWES**
BONNIE **SYLVIA CULLEN**
DENISE **ISOBEL HAYWARD**
ENSEMBLE **ABIGAIL HUGHES**
ANGIE **SASKIA JONES-WALTERS**
FELICITY **MAE MILBURN**
ENSEMBLE **ETTA MUKASA**
PENNY **MARTHA MUKUNGURUTSE**
MISS SPIVAK/MISS BOLDEN/
ENSEMBLE **ELEANOR MYERS**
JANE **INBAL PORT**
MRS BROWN **ARIELLA RIVLIN**
PETER **LIAM ROUSE**
ALBERT **DANIEL SCOTT**
NICKY **LISA SKELTON**
SAMSON **MARTIN TONES**
BELLA **CAROLINE WALKER**
ERIC **ADAM WATSON**

DIRECTOR
GEMMA WOFFINDEN
DESIGNER
EMMA WILLIAMS
LIGHTING AND VIDEO DESIGNER
CHRIS SPEIGHT
ASSISTANT DIRECTOR
KIRSTY PENNYCOOK
STAGE MANAGER
MICHELLE BOOTH
ASSISTANT STAGE MANAGER
CHARLOTTE LARNER
SOUND APPRENTICE
TOBY PEARSON

First Performance:

Courtyard Theatre, West Yorkshire Playhouse, 23 July 2015

WEST YORKSHIRE PLAYHOUSE YOUTH THEATRE

Launched in 2012, the Playhouse Youth Theatre aims to offer young people aged 5–19 the opportunity to explore the world we live in through a range of creative processes, devising work in response to Playhouse productions and commissioning new writing. Our Youth Theatre is passionate about challenging young people and raising aspirations whilst developing skills, knowledge and understanding of young theatre making. We offer a range of performance opportunities, weekly sessions and holiday projects.

West Yorkshire Playhouse Youth Theatre aims to:

- Devise high-quality performance work which gives young people a voice and recognises their talent and creative potential.

- Create performances of both classic and contemporary theatre which draws on the artistic excellence and professional standards of West Yorkshire Playhouse.

- Engage young people through creative sessions, as well as offering participants a range of creative and cultural experiences that will enrich their lives and the lives of their families.

To find out more follow @wyplayhouse #wypyouth
or email youth.theatre@wyp.org.uk

Immune is a play with many twists and turns. Characters experience moments of hope and despair in the turn of a page and this is why it is such an engaging piece of new writing for young audiences.

Drawing on ideas from post-apocalyptic television series and films, graphic novels and popular culture, *Immune* takes its audience into another world. Directing *Immune* with a company of young actors poses many challenges for a range of reasons. At points our production takes on elements of Epic Theatre and at other times you will see performances grounded in naturalism. Not only does the play require the actors to explore themes of mortality and grief, it asks them to move between a range of performance styles and unfamiliar locations whilst telling the story of many complex characters. The notion that a virus has hit your home town, wiped out everyone you know and love, leaving only you and your school friends behind is a frightening concept to consider. As a company we have spent time exploring personal experiences of loss to help the actors engage with the experiences of the characters. We drew pictures, created improvisations and discussed at length who each of the characters would have lost when the virus hit the city. We looked at the arc of the play in relation to the cycle of grief. What are the key events for each character that shape their journey through the play and how does this influence how they respond to each other. It is clear that between Act 1 and Act 2 the characters have reflected on who they are and who they want to be, and like all of us this is influenced by the people around us and how we respond to the challenges in life we face. It was so important that each company member had a sense of how their character changes throughout the play so they could give a truthful performance.

Immune is a dark play with moments of comedy, for example when George is faced with death he says '…if I die will people only remember me a knob head?'. Sadly maybe they will but this is more about how George sees himself in the world. Our production of *Immune* invites the audience to ask themselves – who are you, what is really important to you, how do you want to be remembered and how much of what you do today will shape the answers to these questions?

I have learnt so much from working with such a talented group of young people, the creative team on this show and all the members of production who have helped us to stage *Immune*. Each time I read the play I find something new to consider. The process has been a lot of fun, we did it team, we made a play! Hurrah and thank you all.

WEST YORKSHIRE PLAYHOUSE

West Yorkshire Playhouse in Leeds is a leading UK producing theatre. We are a cultural hub, a place where people gather to tell and share stories and to engage in world class theatre. We make work which is pioneering and relevant, seeking out the best companies and artists to create inspirational theatre in the heart of Yorkshire. From large scale spectacle, to intimate performance we develop and make work for our stages, for found spaces, for touring, for schools and community centres. We create work to entertain and inspire.

As dedicated collaborators, we work regularly with other theatres from across the UK, independent producers, and some of the most distinctive, original voices in theatre today. We develop work with established practitioners and find, nurture and support new voices that ought to be heard. We cultivate new talent by providing creative space for new writers, emerging directors, companies and individual theatre makers to refine their practice.

Alongside our work for the stage we are dedicated to providing creative engagement opportunities that excite and stimulate. We build, run and sustain projects which reach out to everyone from refugee communities, to young people and students, to older communities and people with learning disabilities. At the Playhouse there is always a way to get involved.

West Yorkshire Playhouse – Vital theatre.

Artistic Director **James Brining**

Executive Director **Robin Hawkes**

To find out more about us and our current programme, visit wyp.org.uk, or follow us @WYPlayhouse

Leeds Theatre Trust Limited. Charity No. 255460

VAT No. 545 4890 17 Company No. 926862, England Wales

Registered address Playhouse Square, Quarry Hill, Leeds, LS2 7UP

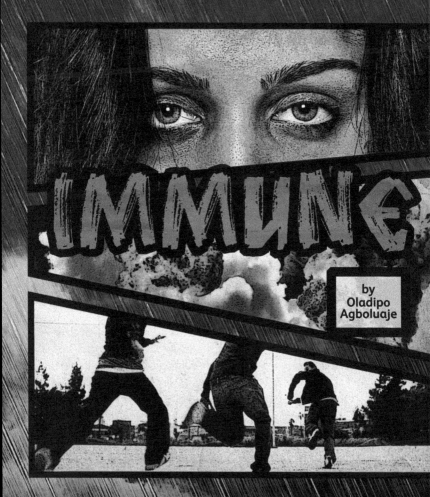

A THEATRE ROYAL PLYMOUTH
YOUNG COMPANY PRODUCTION

IMMUNE

by
Oladipo
Agboluaje

THEATRE
ROYAL
PLYMOUTH

CAST AND CREATIVES

GEORGINA WELSH

EMMA ANDERSON

OWEN WHEATON

OWEN BUSH

MILLIE BOARDMAN

JOHN ARCHER

CHARLIE HEPTINSTALL

AMY WALLACE

MAXINE DENTON

ELSPETH TATE

MITCHELL SIDDONS

GEORGIA WILKINSON

RICHARD TOLMAN

ALEXANDER DOVER

RYAN HOUSE

ALICE CADMORE

MEG DEVEY

DIRECTOR
TIM BELL

ASSISTANT DIRECTOR
CHLOE CADDICK

DESIGNER
JAY KERRY

PRODUCER
JANE PAWSON

PRODUCTION MANAGER
NICK SOPER

LIGHTING DESIGNER
JOHN PERKIS

SOUND DESIGNER
HOLLY HARBOTTLE

AV DESIGNER
MATT HOYLE

STAGE MANAGER
SARAH DONALDSON

COSTUME SUPERVISOR
CHERYL HILL

DEPUTY STAGE MANAGER*
MATTHEW PAIN

ASSISTANT STAGE MANAGER*
JACK HELLEY

AV OPERATOR*
THOMAS MICHAELS

SOUND OPERATOR*
ALICE MCCLEARY

First Performance:
Theatre Royal Plymouth
Wednesday 19 August 2015

* **Young Company Members**

A NOTE FROM THE DIRECTOR TIM BELL

Oladipo Agboluaje puts young people's input at the heart of his creative process. The Theatre Royal Plymouth Young Company has for many years had a brilliant reputation for letting participants lead from the front. This has been a fantastic platform from which we have been able to begin to stage *Immune*. The partnership with the Royal and Derngate and West Yorkshire Playhouse has made this project a richer experience and allowed us to pull in inspiration and creative ideas from each other.

Even at first read, the heightened drama of the play, where the rough and tumble of the school day quickly becomes life and death, requires a playful, eloquent and exhilarating style in order to fully articulate the content. The character's bold choices are echoed in the play's style and structure. Add to this Dipo's love of graphic novels (he's a self-confessed geek), and the beginnings of a diverse theatrical language that matches the play's content starts to emerge. The world of the graphic novel is a rich playground full of possibilities, and it was these concepts that we took into the production.

Rather startling for me, at no point has anyone ever said 'no' to our ideas. Instead, and rather unusually for projects centered on young people, I have been supported by a chorus of professionals who have made our ideas a reality. One of the joys of working at the Theatre Royal Plymouth is that it is a building that celebrates ambition. And nowhere is ambition more unfettered than in a group of young people with the zeal, determination and enterprise of the Young Company. Their ambition knows no bounds, and they have challenged us by setting the bar so high.

THEATRE
ROYAL
PLYMOUTH

The Theatre Royal Plymouth is the largest and best-attended regional producing theatre in the UK and the leading promoter of theatre in the South West. There are three distinctive performance spaces; The Lyric, The Drum and The Lab, as well as an award-winning production and learning centre containing unrivalled set, costume, prop-making and rehearsal facilities.

The Theatre Royal Plymouth produces and presents new plays. It has built a national reputation for the quality of its programme and innovative work, winning the prestigious Peter Brook Empty Space Award, as well producing its own plays, the Theatre Royal Plymouth regularly collaborates with leading theatres and companies in the UK and elsewhere, and provides an exceptional Creative Learning programme with a focus on engaging young and disadvantaged communities.

As part of the Creative Learning programme, the Young Company provides authentic opportunities for young people in Plymouth and the region to engage in a range of activities which reflect and connect with the Theatre's professional programme. This includes script writing, song, dance, theatre design, drama, stage management and direction. There are also weekly workshops in community settings for young people who are not able to access the Young Company without additional support. These groups run as part of the broader Young Company, collaborating through productions, celebration events and joint projects. The Theatre's specialist work with vulnerable young people such as refugees and asylum seekers and those with disabilities is also closely connected with the Young Company.

In light of its focus on new writing and extensive work with young people, Theatre Royal Plymouth is committed to exploring innovative ways of creating new plays for young people to perform.

Chief Executive **Adrian Vinken**
Artistic Director **Simon Stokes**

To find out more about our current programme please visit
www.theatreroyal.com or follow us @TRPlymouth

Characters

JANE

PETER

NICHOLAS

CRAIG

DENISE

SAMSON

BELLA

BONNIE

PENNY

GEORGE

ANGIE

ERIC

ALBERT

FELICITY

MISS SPIVAK, MR. BROWN, MISS BOLDEN, MISS SMITH, MR COLLIER

RADIO 1, RADIO 2

Where there is no dialogue after the name of the character, e.g.

FELICITY:

it means the character does not reply. You can either mark the moment as an active silence according to the emotion of the characters or skip over it to the next speaker.

/ signifies a speaker being interrupted by the next speaker.

... signifies a trailing off of speech.

ACT ONE

St. John's Academy, Monday morning. By the school gate.

A bunch of school mates play rough.

SAMSON: It's an ordinary day.

CRAIG: An ordinary school day.

SAMSON: Monday's come too soon.

ALBERT: It's the first cold day of the warmest year since records began. I just want to put my back to a radiator. I'll worry about global warming once I'm all toasty. But first I've got to get myself past these muckers!

ALBERT joins in the rough and tumble.

SAMSON: Miss Spivak! Miss Spivak!

CRAIG: And we're through the gate and passing through the glass door entrance to St. John's Academy.

ALBERT: Good morning, Miss Spivak.

SAMSON: Good morning, Miss.

SPIVAK: Coats off

No fizzy drinks or crisps

Albert, tuck in your shirt

Samson. Are those trainers you're wearing?

ALBERT: Yes, Miss

CRAIG: Aw, Miss

7

ALBERT: Yes, Miss

SAMSON: No, Miss

CRAIG: Miss Spivak says she's eager to see what we come up with for Friday's Creativity Day. I reply with something smart.

SPIVAK: Do you always have to be so cheeky, Craig?

CRAIG: Can't help myself, Miss.

ALBERT: Inside the glass doors there is the usual coming together and splitting of groups like atoms.

PENNY: We watch out for Bonnie who's talking to Eric because Angie is gossiping about her Dad.

ALBERT: Eric is smiling but Bonnie is not. Bonnie is looking at our group because she knows Angie is talking about her.

BELLA: I smile as Peter preaches to me about Jesus. I'm only listening because like half the girls in school I fancy him: Peter, not Jesus. And he's telling me how God is way above the bigotries that people try to taint Him with.

PENNY: I'm laughing inside watching Bella act like she's interested and I'm thinking, a few words about Jesus for a moment with Peter, I could just about handle it.

ANGIE reveals some spicy gossip.

No! He didn't!

GEORGE, drinking from a carton of orange juice, walks up to ERIC.

ERIC: Here goes...

So, Bonnie, what are you doing on/

George spills juice all over my shirt. My weekend spent summoning up courage, of talking to my reflection in the mirror, ruined.

You idiot!

GEORGE: Sorry, mate. Didn't see you there.

ANGIE: Oh but Eric is having none of it, because George is grinning like he did it on purpose and because George and Eric do not get on anymore.

ERIC: And all I see is his stupid grin.

ERIC shoves GEORGE.

GEORGE: Hey!

GEORGE shoves ERIC back.

SAMSON: Oh, it's kicking off.

CRAIG: My money's on Eric.

ALBERT: George all day every day.

SAMSON: Mr. Brown! Mr. Brown!

Boring, boring Mr. Brown.

BROWN: What's going on here?

GEORGE and ERIC stop shoving each other.

GEORGE: Nothing, sir.

ERIC: Just two friends messing about, sir.

CRAIG: George and Eric promise to meet behind the shed after school.

ALBERT: Mr. Brown does not hear this promise.

DENISE: If he had he would have told them that some promises can be broken, which is the opposite of Mr. Smith who says promises are debts that must be paid.

SAMSON: And so boring Mr. Brown with his boring voice reminds us not to be late for his boring chemistry class.

BROWN: We'll be conducting an experiment, chemicals and Bunsen burners. You're all looking forward to that, eh?

ALL: *(Except CRAIG.) Boring.*

CRAIG: Yes!

ALBERT: And Nicholas thumps Craig in the back.

CRAIG: Ow!

ANGELA: God knows why you're so keen on chemistry.

CRAIG: Because I'm going to...

ANGIE: Oh really? How exciting.

Why does Craig think I care about how many times he's seen *Batman Returns*, or about how he's going to make a Scarecrow's fear gas of his own?

Uh-huh, uh-huh.

CRAIG: I'll make only one dose just for you, Nicola.

NICHOLAS: Call me Nicola again I'll break your arm.

CRAIG: Scared already.

See how he feels when he confronts his greatest fear. See how he feels when I make his life a misery. See how he feels having to hide during lunch break. See how/

ANGIE turns her back on CRAIG to continue gossiping to the rest.

ANGIE: Yeah, yeah. So like I was saying, Bonnie's Dad and Felicity...

PENNY: *(Warning.)* Felicity's coming.

ANGIE: In mid-sentence I switch.

So who watched the show last night?

PENNY: But there's no point. Felicity knows we're talking about her.

DENISE: Felicity doesn't care what people think of her.

SAMSON: Felicity doesn't care about anything, not even herself.

ALBERT: Angie, are you sure you saw Felicity buying beer at The Pilgrim's Progress on Saturday night?

ANGIE: I saw her with my own two eyes.

ALBERT: Let's ask Bonnie if she knows her Dad sells beer to school kids.

ERIC: *(Rubbing at the orange stain.)* Albert, doesn't stupid ever take a day off with you? Why would you ask her that?

And he's pissing me off more than usual because this orange stain won't come off. And I'm looking at Bonnie and I know I should go wash it off in the toilet but I can't move because Bonnie hasn't answered the question I never got to ask her. And I know she knows what I was going to say.

ALBERT: Denise who is smarter than all of us tells Eric, go wash your shirt in the toilet. And Eric trips over my foot because he's looking at Bonnie. And it's obvious to me that she's not interested in him so who's stupid now?

PENNY: Everybody thinks Denise is smart but she only says the obvious thing before anyone else. She asks the obvious question before anyone else. Not this time.

Why doesn't/

DENISE: Why doesn't Felicity buy her beer at the off license instead?

PENNY: *(Fumes at DENISE.)* Jane's here. She interrupts Bella who is laughing at a joke Peter did not make about Jesus, which is stupid because everyone knows you can only make jokes about Mohammed.

BONNIE: The only good thing about Jane being here is that she shuts up Angie's big mouth. I know she's talking about my Dad but she'll deny it if I take her up on it.

JANE: Get into your groups. Hurry up people.

They divide themselves as follows:

Group One (dance) – NICHOLAS, CRAIG, DENISE.

Group Two (song) – SAMSON, BELLA, BONNIE, PENNY

Group Three (video) – GEORGE, ANGIE, ALBERT, FELICITY. ERIC joins them on his return from the toilet.

PENNY: You'd think she was Miss Spivak the way she carries on.

SAMSON: But we don't argue. We've only got ten minutes before we head to our classes.

PENNY: Friday won't take care of itself. So it's up to Peter and Jane, the Student Organizers.

ANGIE: Peter and Jane who've been best friends since primary school.

BONNIE: Peter and Jane who used to be more than just friends if not for someone's big mouth.

PENNY: Peter and Jane, the golden couple, handpicked by Miss Bolden, Miss Bolden who likes a quick fix to every problem.

ALBERT: Miss Bolden who doesn't waste time asking for volunteers.

SAMSON: Miss Bolden who picks her A team for each and every show. There is no room for growing into your own in Miss Bolden's class.

PENNY: *(Mimics MISS BOLDEN.)* 'That's how it works in the real world, people. It's either you've got it or you haven't.'

And Peter and Jane have it in spades. Good for them. Who wants to be the class dogsbody?

CRAIG: Peter and Jane whisper to themselves.

NICHOLAS: Christ, Jane's looking our way.

DENISE: Don't look at her!

JANE: Group One. The dance. Let's see it.

NICHOLAS: Craig! You idiot!

DENISE: What, now?

JANE: You left rehearsals early yesterday. Peter and I came back and you'd gone.

PETER: We need to report on your progress to Miss Bolden.

JANE: You must take your responsibility seriously. Our families and friends will be in the audience. The local councillor will be there too. We may not be going for a competition but you still represent the school...

ALBERT: Blah, blah, blah...

JANE: ...It was irresponsible of you leaving rehearsals like that...

PENNY: I'm smart enough not to say that's because you two went AWOL and time was up and our parents were waiting because then you'd ask why no one came to look for you.

BONNIE: If I'd known Jane would be running Creativity Day I wouldn't have volunteered.

ANGIE: I'll never believe a word Miss Bolden says again. She told us this time we'd all have a chance at being Student Organizers. The others might not think it but I am up for taking charge every now and then.

NICHOLAS: But Craig starts to hum the tune. And he's looking at me and smiling with the teeth I'm going to knock out during lunch break, the little turd. It's a good thing Denise won't follow his lead.
DENISE taps her feet. NICHOLAS glares at her. She shrugs.

NICHOLAS: Denise!

So I've got to join in, haven't I?

Music. They clap out a rhythm and dance to it. NICHOLAS has a hard time keeping to the beat.

NICHOLAS: And Craig is calling me Nicola and telling me to keep to the beat. And I can hear the sniggers. Don't worry, Craig. At lunch break, you're mine.

They finish dancing.

JANE: Group Two, you left early as well.

BONNIE: We left on time. You two didn't come back from your meeting. We couldn't hang around waiting for you.

GEORGE: Stand off. Not because Bonnie isn't saying what we're all thinking.

DENISE: *(Watches BELLA.)* Not because Bonnie is afraid of Jane. She isn't.

ALBERT: But in the way she says 'you two' and 'your meeting'. You don't need to be told they hate each other.

ANGIE: And the reason they hate each other is one of those I don't know why but I think it was when she said she did and she said she did and I'm not sure but ask her who's also not sure because she wasn't there but heard it from him who heard it from them. Yeah, one of those kind of reasons.

CRAIG: Before harsh words are drawn Peter the peace-maker comes between them.

ANGIE: I hate Christians. They are killjoys.

PETER: Let's hear you, Group Two.

SAMSON: We haven't finished.

PETER: Give us whatever you've got. Quickly.

PENNY: We'll show you this evening at rehearsal.

PETER: Miss Bolden needs to know where you are with this.

BONNIE: We said we'll show you this evening, all right?

BELLA claps a beat and sways, to the anger of PENNY, SAMSON and BONNIE.

15

SAMSON: Bella.

PENNY: Anything to get inside Peter's good books.

BONNIE: Anything to get inside Peter's Y-fronts.

PENNY: Anything to... What am I saying? I fancy Peter myself.

PENNY joins in.

SAMSON and BONNIE give PENNY a look. PENNY shrugs an apology. BONNIE joins in. They clap and sway, except for SAMSON who only claps.

PENNY: And it isn't so bad...

BELLA: Samson, move your legs, will you?

Everybody wants to sing their song

How can they sing it

When the words are all wrong

It's A-Okay, it's A-Okay

JANE: Stop! Just stop.

BELLA: It's not that bad.

PENNY: We're getting there.

SAMSON: Move my legs to that crap. Please.

BONNIE: We don't care what you think.

JANE: Group Three, please.

BELLA: Peter, what do you think/

JANE: Group Three, your phones.

ANGIE, GEORGE and ALBERT slowly bring out their phones.

ANGIE: Miss Tolworth, English teacher, zooming by makes a pit stop to remind us about school policy on using mobile phones.

SAMSON: *(Dreamily.)* Miss Tolworth...

PETER: It's for Friday, Miss.

SAMSON: And my eyes follow her to the lift that's for staff only that takes her up to the staff room on level three.

JANE: Group Three, we're waiting.

NICHOLAS: *(Surprised.)* George goes first.

CRAIG: Giggles.

PENNY: Followed by more giggles.

CRAIG: Giggles drowned by gasps of surprise as George swipes his phone.

BELLA: Even Peter raises an eyebrow.

They huddle around GEORGE to see the video.

PETER: The video is of George standing by Charles Church.

JANE: He gives a potted history of the ruin. He tells us what he loves about this town.

DENIS: And after, his hopes for the future.

GEORGE: I want to study engineering at university, here or anywhere else. I want to marry shortly after and have kids. I've always dreamed of living in New York. But I know if I do go to New York or anywhere else I'll always come back.

JANE: A stunned second of silence that in our consciousness lasts an eternity.

17

PETER: George is not known for sentiment.

BELLA: George is not known for doing his homework.

ALBERT: George is not known for doing anything but getting into fights and being a knob head.

PETER: Eric breaks the silence by yawning louder than an elephant trumpeting a heavy metal anthem.

ANGIE: Eric who has come back from the toilet to piss on George's parade.

GEORGE: Don't worry, mate. End of school day. My fists are going to rain all over your face.

ERIC: You reckon?

JANE: Eric, you're next. Eric!

ERIC: What?

JANE: Your video.

SAMSON: Eric doesn't bring out his phone. Eric has not shot his video.

PETER: Eric, Friday is only four days away.

ERIC:

JANE: Eric, we promised Mr. Smith the films would be ready by today.

PETER: Mr. Smith only has Period Three today to help us edit them.

SAMSON: Mr. Smith won't be happy. Mr. Smith likes promises to be kept.

JANE: What about you, Albert?

ALBERT: Sorry.

ANGIE: I've done mine.

JANE: Albert. We let you off early yesterday.

ALBERT: I went to the navy base. They wouldn't let me in.

JANE: Did you?

ALBERT: I swear.

JANE: OK.

    Liar.

ALBERT: It's true!

JANE: I said, OK. Albert.

    Liar.

ALBERT: I'll shoot one in school during lunch break. I
promise.

ANGIE: I've done mine.

JANE: Felicity? How about you?

FELICITY:

JANE: I'll take it that's a no, then?

FELICITY:

ANGIE: I've done mine.

CRAIG: Jane used to go out with Eric when Eric was a good
boy.

BELLA: When Jane was going out with Peter.

PENNY: And Angie told.

SAMSON: And Peter found out.

BELLA: And Peter hasn't forgiven Jane.

PENNY: And Jane hasn't forgiven Angie.

CRAIG: Eric now is as big a knob head as George. But I'd never say that to his face. *(Looks at NICHOLAS.)* I've got my own knob head to deal with.

ANGIE: I've done mine.

JANE: This bunch of idiots.

This is a chance to prove we can organize an event on this scale on our own and you're not taking this serious/

PETER: Jane, Angie says she's done hers.

ANGIE: And Jane looks at me like I'm some kind of something. And I'm thinking, why should I bother, but I want people to see my hope for the future.

Here goes...

So this is me/

The school bell rings.

GEORGE: We say yes, let's meet during lunch break.

PENNY: Am I the only one miffed that we're rehearsing in Period Five anyway?

DENISE: No but Friday is only four days away, so.

PENNY: Oh shut up.

Chemistry class. The students huddle around MR. BROWN.

BROWN: Albert, open the windows.

ALBERT: It's cold, sir.

BROWN: You know we must open the windows before we conduct any experiment. I don't want a repeat of last time.

ALBERT: I'm freezing.

BROWN: Samson, the windows.

SAMSON: You asked Albert, first.

Boring, boring, Mr. Brown.

DENISE: Everyone waits for Peter to open the windows.

PETER: I'd have opened the windows but you should have seen Eric and George going at it in English. And so I stay put to keep them apart. If only Bella would stop playing with her hair...

JANE: I would have opened the windows but I hate chemistry class. This is the one class where Peter takes full responsibility.

BELLA: Peter is eyeing me up. Nice.

PETER: ...If Mr. Brown lights the burner...

CRAIG: I love chemistry but Mr. Brown is the only man of science who makes me believe in magic. Mr. Brown can turn excitement into boredom.

Giggles.

BROWN: Are you being a smartarse again, Craig?

CRAIG: Me, sir? No sir.

NICHOLAS pokes CRAIG in the back of the head.

ALBERT: And I really want to ask Bonnie about her Dad. I can't ask Felicity. She never talks. She's not even here.

BONNIE: I thought Eric wanted to ask me out. He didn't look at me once in English class. And I'd have said yes and I would have told Jane where to go. I'd have said Eric's dumped you for me so you can talk down to me how you like but it doesn't change the fact I'm with Eric and Peter won't have you back. And... Are Penny and Angie still going on about my Dad?

NICHOLAS pokes CRAIG in the back of the head.

ERIC: I can't look at Bonnie because I know people are thinking she blew me off. I never got to ask her and she never got back to me and I'll get you for this George.

GEORGE: Didn't think Eric would get so het up about this morning but I'm not backing down. Not in a million years.

JANE: Mr. Brown is talking about chemical reactions, interrupting himself several times to remind us to keep our protective goggles on, to again tell Albert and Samson to open the windows or we won't conduct the experiment with the volatile liquids and for Nicholas to stop poking Craig in the head. And I'm wondering why Peter doesn't open the windows.

DENISE: Why doesn't Peter open the windows?

PETER: I bet they're wondering why I don't open the windows.

BONNIE: And Mr. Brown tells Angie and Penny to stop talking and pay attention to what he's saying.

NICHOLAS pokes CRAIG in the back of the head.

BROWN: Nicholas! If you poke Craig one more time...

NICHOLAS: I didn't touch him, sir.

Oh yeah, you can see me poking Craig's head but you don't haul him up for taking the piss out of you.

And I'm wondering why Peter doesn't open the windows.

JANE: *(Horrified.)* Mr. Brown has forgotten himself and is about to light the burner.

PETER: Bella!

BROWN: Bella, stop flicking your hair or I'll move you to the back of the class.

JANE: *(Looks at her watch.)* Come on, Time. What are you waiting for?

NICHOLAS: Mr. Brown explains his experiment. I poke Craig in the back of the head.

CRAIG: Mr. Brown sees my head jerk forward.

BROWN: Nicholas, did you poke Craig again?

NICHOLAS: No, sir. Did I, Craig?

BROWN: Craig?

CRAIG: Mum's words ring in my ear. The only way to beat a bully is to stand up to them. But I so want to drop Nicholas in it. I so want to say, he's picking on me.

No, sir.

JANE: No one's listening to Mr. Brown because Eric and George are at it.

PETER: It's a low level conflict, baiting each other from the distance I put between them with four letter word tit for tats.

Enough, you two. Mr. Brown will hear you.

SAMSON: Penny is talking to Angie who is not listening because she wants the inside scoop on Eric and George.

BONNIE: I'm wondering if Angie and Penny are talking about me and now is the right time to face Angie.

MR BROWN: Craig, come to the front.

Shuffle. Rearrange.

Bella, to the back. If you can't do as I tell you...

BELLA: I hate being told what to do so I move as slowly as I can. But I'll be closer to Peter. No, no! Take your time. Don't want it to look like you're desperate, not after this morning.

MR BROWN: Quickly, Bella. Will someone open the window?

PETER: Eric and George won't dare kick off in Mr. Brown's class. We've wasted so much time. I'd better go open the windows.

BELLA: *(Reacts to PETER walking past her.)* What the...

PETER: Eric and George swallow up the space I have vacated.

CRAIG: Two volatile chemicals reacting.

ANGIE: Penny keeps talking and I'm like, hey, Penny, shut up! I can't hear Eric and George with you barking in my ear.

JANE: Before the pot boils over, Mr. Brown yells at them. The bass of his voice, a voice that says I've had it with your Tear Ten class, freezes us for a second.

CRAIG: And in the silence of that second I say something snarky to Nicholas.

NICHOLAS: I say something back to him but Craig is great with one-liners and I'm not. And everyone's laughing at me. Even Eric and George, and Saint Peter takes a moment to look at me like he's saying, he got you mate. He got you real good.

CRAIG: I got him real good, Mum. I put him in his place.

MR BROWN: Quiet please! Bella! I told you to move to the back.

CRAIG: I got him real good!

ALL: Laugh, laugh, laugh, laugh, laugh.

NICHOLAS: I lunge at the little turd.

CRAIG: I throw my arm out of his reach and over go the chemicals. One into another, hiss and fumes. Scarecrow gas.

Smoke fills the stage.

PETER: Everyone is coughing and screaming, until Mr. Brown and I open the windows.

JANE: And the smoke clears like a miracle.

SAMSON: Craig!

CRAIG: It was an accident!

DENISE: And soon we are breathing all right.

25

BROWN: Is everybody OK?

PENNY: I'm fine, sir.

ANGIE: I'm all right, sir.

JANE: Mr. Brown will have to log in another incident. Mr. Brown will have to have us checked out.

DENISE: Craig you idiot. You nearly got us killed.

CRAIG: It was Nicholas/

NICHOLAS: Me? You knocked over the chemicals. You were going to throw them over me.

CRAIG: I was not!

BROWN: Shut up, the both of you!

DENISE: If Albert and Samson refused to, someone else should have opened the windows.

They turn to PETER.

PETER: Don't look at me.

I should have opened the windows.

BROWN: Good, well if everyone's all right/

JANE: And Bella starts to scream.

BONNIE: We turn to see Bella lying on the floor clutching her hair. Her hair dyed with chemicals.

CRAIG: Oh god. Oh god. It was an accident.

PETER: God forgive me.

JANE: Mr Brown looks like someone's who's been handed his P45. He carries Bella in his arms and races through the door.

ALBERT: Felicity. Have you been here all along?

Lunch Break.

ANGIE: You should have been there.

DENISE: We wait for Peter and Jane. We form puddles discussing the breaking news of the 'chemical attack' on the school.

ANGIE: We were coughing and coughing.

BONNIE: Angie has something else to talk about.

DENISE: And Albert being Albert is flexible with the truth.

ALBERT: It went up like a mushroom cloud.

ANGIE: We all had to go to medical.

DENISE: And for once they're wishing they were in Mr. Brown's class.

ALBERT: Everyone's skin turned yellow. We all had to be quarantined.

SAMSON: Do you think Craig really tried to gas Nicholas? He could have turned him into a nervous wreck and have him sent to Arkham Asylum.

DENISE: Don't be daft. Arkham Asylum isn't real.

SAMSON: I don't argue with Denise because Denise is smart.

PENNY: She didn't answer the real question: did Craig try to get Nicholas?

ALBERT: I left Eric in the dining hall.

SAMSON: What's the point of waiting? We should just go.

DENISE: Has anyone seen George?

PENNY: And Craig? Nicholas was looking for him. I told him not to forget we were meeting.

PENNY: Craig is in medical with a counsellor.

PENNY: That's one way of hiding from Nicholas.

ALBERT: It was like acid and it's eaten away all her hair and half the side of her face. She looks like Two-Face.

SAMSON: Felicity is not coming. I saw her go out the school gate and head for the town centre.

BONNIE: I know what they're thinking. Angie glances at me but carries on telling her version of events in chemistry class. She knows I'm watching her. She wouldn't dare...

ALBERT: Bonnie, is it true your Dad sells alcohol to under-16s?

BONNIE: Who told you that? If you spread lies about my father I will report you to Miss Spivak.

ALBERT walks away from BONNIE.

PENNY: Miss Spivak who has warned us about spreading rumours about one another, even if they are true.

ANGIE: Bonnie's shouting at Albert but looking straight at me.

PENNY: Albert. Are you stupid?

ALBERT: What?

PENNY: You asked Bonnie about Felicity.

ALBERT: I didn't.

PENNY: Why are you lying? Everyone saw you.

ALBERT: Jane turns up. Followed by Peter. What a saviour.

JANE: I wasn't expecting anyone to turn up.

ANGIE: I was here first Jane.

PETER: How are you all feeling?

ANGIE: I'm A-OK, Jane.

PENNY: The others aren't coming. Can we go?

JANE: No.

PENNY: We're meeting in Period Five anyway.

JANE: No.

PETER: Any more work on the song, Group Two?

SAMSON: No.

JANE: I've spoken to the cover teacher. He's agreed to let you work on the song during music class. Peter will pop in to check on you.

PETER: Angie, you were about to show us your video this morning.

ANGIE: Wish we're all here. No matter. Friday's the big day. Out comes my phone.

There's me by the Hoe, facing the Sound. Do I love this city or what? Cut away to me looking up at Francis Drake's statue. I want to be hairdresser to the stars. I'll have plenty of affairs with Hollywood A-listers and then I'll go into politics.

ALBERT: Awkward silences are the best, aren't they?

ANGIE: What I'm saying is I'll live my life to the fullest.

SAMSON: Well, you'll certainly put the ho' in Hoe.

ANGIE: Shut up.

PETER: It's not bad, with some careful editing...

ANGIE: This is about me. This is about my hopes for the future.

PETER: There are things best kept to yourself, Angie.

ANGIE: Not the reaction I was expecting but I don't care. I don't care. I don't care.

The bell rings. End of break.

JANE: See you in Period Five. Please don't be late.

BONNIE: As we head back to class I'm like, this is what Karma feels like, Angie. See what it feels like having everyone talking about your business.

JANE: Before you go, Peter. We must fix a time to write the programme for Friday.

PETER: I was thinking we should postpone the Day.

JANE: The Year Nines are building the set this afternoon.

PETER: It's the right thing to do. We're not ready anyway.

JANE: We would have been ready if you hadn't snuck off yesterday. I gave Miss Bolden my word that we could handle the festival on our own.

PETER: With Bella in the hospital...

JANE: There's nothing you can do for Bella.

PETER: I should have opened the window.

JANE: You want to be there for everyone, Peter? How about being here for me? (*Makes to leave.*) Don't forget to check on the media class as well.

PETER: Jane I/

A roar from students.

STUDENTS: Fight! Fight! Fight! Fight! Fight!

JANE: The cheering is coming from behind the shed. Mr. Collier, the PE teacher, races past us.

PETER: We get there just in time to see him tearing George and Eric off each other.

ANGIE: They couldn't wait for after school.

PETER: Mr Collier marches them to the clinic. From there he'll take them to Miss Spivak. From there they will be sent to Period Five detention with Miss Tolworth. Their parents will be informed and they will be suspended.

JANE: I want to scream, you can't ruin my show. But I remember who I am. I remain calm. I turn to Peter.

Pity you weren't there to save them.

And I know it's unfair, it's not his fault and he's doubting himself but it's all I can say to stop myself from tipping over the edge. At the end of the day, deep down, Peter is strong. He can take it. Peter has God.

PETER: And I want to say, you're right, Jane. I care too much about other people. I don't want to take part in the Day anymore. I want to look after my soul before putting the welfare of others first. Instead I watch Jane head back into the building. And not for the first time I'm trying to figure out the difference between cowardice and forbearance.

Rehearsal studio, Period Five.

Thumping sounds are heard throughout the scene.

The others clap in rhythm to a beat as Group One dances. CRAIG is subdued.

JANE: This is a vast improvement on this morning.

NICHOLAS: Thank you.

JANE: Group Two. Let's hear you.

Thump.

PENNY: Do they have to make such a racket? We can hear them from up here.

JANE: They'll soon finish building the set. Don't let it bother you.

Thump.

Come on.

Buoyed by Group One's performance, Group Two psych themselves up. They sing boisterously. Their enthusiasm infects their mates who join in clapping and dancing along:

> Everyone wants to sing their song
>
> How can they sing it
>
> When the words are all wrong
>
> It's A-Okay
>
> It's A-Okay

You've found your voice

Now let it sing out

This is your moment

Let's hear you shout

It's A-Okay

It's A-Okay

The others cheer.

BONNIE: We're still working on it. Mr. Moore gave us some great ideas.

Thump.

JANE: Brilliant.

Friday's going to be great.

Group Three.

ALBERT: Oh no.

JANE: Come on, Group Three. We've seen one and a half of you.

ANGIE: Oh thanks.

PETER: Unless you made another video during lunch break, Angie?

ANGIE: You patronizing/

JANE: Felicity's not here. Let's have you, Albert.

ALBERT: As agreed, Angie and I turn to Peter.

PETER: I want to speak. But when I met them in media class I told them they'd have to explain themselves. It's so simple. All they have to do is open their mouths and say it. I told them yet Albert and Angie are looking at me. Goody two-shoes Peter to lighten their load, Saint Peter to bear their cross.

JANE: Well?

ANGIE & ALBERT: Peter?

      Peter?

      Peter!

JANE: It's obvious they still haven't done it. But I'm not letting them off.

Will one of you say something?

Thump.

ANGIE & ALBERT: Peter. Please.

PETER: And so I tell Jane that Angie has refused to reshoot her video and that Albert didn't shoot his video during lunch break like he promised. And that Mr. Smith was so angry he's told them to edit the video themselves.

JANE: What?

ANGIE: It's OK. We know what to do.

JANE: But you haven't shot your films.

ALBERT: I'll go shoot something around the school now. It'll only take a few minutes.

PETER: See if you can get Miss Tolworth to release Eric early from detention so he can go with you.

ALBERT: Miss Tolworth...

JANE: Angie, go with Albert.

ANGIE: I'm not changing mine.

JANE: Yes you are. Go on.

ANGIE: What's her problem? But I know her problem and her problem is me. And I so want us to be friends again and so I go with Albert.

ANGIE and ALBERT exit.

JANE: The rest of you, keep rehearsing. If you need us give us a shout.

The groups rehearse. JANE draws PETER to one side.

ALBERT: Didn't think the other groups would have moved on.

JANE: Why didn't you tell me about Group Three sooner?

PETER: They can speak for themselves.

ANGIE: What is wrong with my video?

ALBERT: Nothing, if you're shooting a porno.

ANGIE thumps ALBERT on the shoulder.

Ow!

Thump.

JANE: Is this about this afternoon?

PETER: Let's do this outside.

JANE: We do this here.

Thump.

ALBERT: Those Year Nines...

ANGIE: Did you see that?

ALBERT: See what?

ANGIE: Albert. Look...

PETER: Fine. I quit.

> *Thump.*

> *The class erupts.*

- You can't quit!

- We've only got four days left!

- I'm not taking your place.

- Lover's tiff.

- We know you were together on Sunday.

- Kiss and make up.

> *ANGIE and ALBERT burst into the room, in panic.*

ANGIE: Come outside!

JANE: What?

ANGIE: Come outside. Now!

PETER: The panic in their voices.

DENISE: It says we're not playing.

JANE: We are outside the rehearsal studio.

> I can't see anything.

DENISE: What is it?

PETER: The rehearsal studio is on the third floor, the top floor of the academy, the same floor as the staff room.

JANE: Only staff can use the lift. But this is Period Five and so no one minds. There aren't many of us around.

ALBERT: Period Five is for remedial classes.

SAMSON: And for students like us doing extra-curricular activities.

PETER: And for teachers who don't like taking work home.

CRAIG: And for students serving detention.

SAMSON: And for Miss Spivak who is always the last to leave.

ALBERT: Look down.

PETER: I can't see anything.

ANGIE: Look at the stairs.

DENICE: Is that Miss Tolworth lying there?

ALBERT: Miss Tolworth!

JANE: Why didn't you call for help?

BONNIE screams.

PETER: There are more bodies. By the lift, on the other floors, in the class rooms, on the ground floor.

JANE: Is this a joke?

NICHOLAS: What is going on?

CRAIG: Oh my God, oh my God, oh my God.

DENISE: Let's, let's go.

SAMSON: Go where?

DENISE: Downstairs. We can't stay up here.

PETER: We walk down the stairs past prone bodies to the ground floor because we're too afraid to take the lift. Angie starts to sob. So does Samson.

PENNY: Denise who has all the answers has no answer this time.

ALBERT: Peter, the rock, is shaking like a leaf.

JANE: Samson is stuck on the second floor, unable to command his legs to keep up with the rest of us.

Samson, come downstairs!

PETER: The thump-thump-thumping.

BONNIE: They were bodies falling from the upper floors.

ALBERT: They look like jigsaw pieces.

SAMSON: This is why I cannot move. This is why I am stuck on the second floor.

JANE: Samson, you don't want whatever's affected these people to affect you while you're up there.

Peter and Albert go up to help Samson down one step at a time.

CRAIG: I head to Miss Spivak's office.

BONNIE: We all jump as Eric and George tumble out of the detention room on the ground floor.

ERIC: What's happened?

PETER: We don't know.

GEORGE: You're all right.

NICHOLAS: So are you.

ERIC: Miss Tolworth popped upstairs to the staff room. She never came back.

ERIC and GEORGE see MISS TOLWORTH's body.

ERIC: Miss Tolworth...

CRAIG returns from MISS SPIVAK's office.

PETER: Craig, is Miss Spivak all right?

He shakes his head.

ERIC: What do we do?

DENISE: We can't stay here. This place is infected.

NICHOLAS: Infected with what?

DENISE: I don't know. Don't look at me.

JANE: And everyone's on their phone.

ANGIE: Mum.

BONNIE: Dad.

SAMSON: I'm not moving from here.

PETER: Please, let's not panic.

GEORGE: Do you have a better idea?

DENISE: I call 999. I hang up and redial 999.

ALBERT: Peter, is this the Apocalypse? Is this the end times?

PETER: I don't know.

ALBERT: You must know!

PETER: I don't know!

DENISE: I hang up and redial 999.

ERIC: Mum.

GEORGE: Dad.

SAMSON: Pick up the phone.

CRAIG: Answer, for God's sake.

ALBERT: Pick up the phone!

> *A frenzy of calls to families, friends and acquaintances. We hear a variety of ringtones and voicemail messages.*

ALL: Hello?

> Hello?

> Hello?

DENISE: Is this happening elsewhere?

GEORGE: The TV. There might be something on the telly.

JANE: The media room. We try not to look at the two Year Eleven students slumped over the tables.

GEORGE: Nothing. No breaking news.

ERIC: Life going on as usual.

JANE: No one knows what's happened here.

ALBERT: Why is no one answering their phone?

DENISE: For goodness' sake we've got to go outside.

BONNIE: What about our mates?

GEORGE: What about our teachers?

PETER: There's nothing we can do for them now.

JANE: And I'm glad Peter said it and not me.

SAMSON: And I'm glad Peter said it and not me.

CRAIG: And I'm glad Peter said it and not me.

PETER: The glass doors open and we walk out into the first cold day of the warmest year since records began.

JANE: And it feels much colder.

End of Act One

Act Two

Towards the town centre.

PETER: Has anyone been able to contact their parents?

An uneasy silence.

SAMSON: I want to go home.

JANE: You can't go home.

SAMSON: Why not?

JANE: Because...!

> And I want to say, 'you saw the bodies along the way. You
> heard no one answer Peter,' but I see the look in his eyes
> and I can't tell him the obvious, your parents are dead,
> then it means my parents are dead. And I'm thinking this
> is what you get when you crave responsibility, people will
> either despise you or they'll burden you with their issues
> but I'm not ready for this.

> Look, we're almost at the town centre. There must be
> someone else who's survived.

SAMSON: I'm going home.

JANE: How will you get home?

SAMSON: I'll walk.

JANE: Get back here! We are not splitting up the group now
walk this way! Move!

PETER: Jane...

JANE: Just leave it, Peter.

The town centre.

PETER: We're here!

The town centre. Someone must have survived somehow. And someone must know why we survived because we've asked that question and not even Denise knows the answer, and God hasn't spoken to me. God, please, someone, just one man or woman... Oh my God...

ANGIE: Bodies.

GEORGE: Bodies everywhere.

DENISE: I expected as much but still...

PENNY: And Denise is looking like death warmed up. She is speechless like the rest of us.

SAMSON: I'm crying.

PETER: Hello?

JANE: Hello!

DENISE: Is there anybody here?

SAMSON: Bodies everywhere.

GEORGE: The high street, the police station, the shopping centre.

ANGIE: What do we do now?

CRAIG: I'm thinking what everyone is thinking but not saying. If they won't say it I won't say it.

PETER: And no one has phoned back.

PENNY: No.

JANE: No one.

ERIC: Nothing from Twitter.

GEORGE: Nothing from Facebook.

BONNIE: No hashtag.

ERIC: No comments.

PENNY: Not even a 'like' for the pictures we posted.

ANGELA: Are we the only ones alive?

PETER: Let's not think about that now.

PENNY: Where do we go now?

SAMSON: I want my Mum and Dad. They're not like these
    kids. They'll know what to do. But my legs won't move.

BONNIE: My Dad's pub is round the corner.

JANE: I don't think that's a good idea, Bonnie.

BONNIE: Don't tell me what to do.

JANE: I'm just saying/

BONNIE: Just because Eric dumped you for me.

JANE: Bonnie!

BONNIE: He was going to ask me out. That's why you've been
    giving me grief, you spiteful, overbearing bitch!

JANE: But I didn't even know you and Eric...

BONNIE: Get out of my face!

ERIC: She said yes.

PETER: I lead Jane away from Bonnie.

JANE: I've broken up with Eric, anyway. Bonnie, don't!

PETER: Leave her, Jane.

DENISE: Jane whispers to Peter. She doesn't want Bonnie to hear. But I know what she is saying.

JANE: She phoned, he didn't pick up. Don't let her go in there.

DENISE: I'm thinking it.

ALBERT: I'm thinking it.

SAMSON: I'm looking at Bonnie heading for the door and I'm thinking it.

GEORGE: Eric's eyes are lit up for Bonnie. But he must be thinking it.

ERIC: She said yes.

CRAIG: I know they're all thinking it but they won't say it.

NICHOLAS: Isn't anyone going to say it? We're all thinking it.

GEORGE: I was a prat for spilling juice on Eric. I did it on purpose. I can't remember why we stopped being friends. I'm looking straight at him but he won't look at me.

ERIC: All I can see is Bonnie at the door of The Pilgrim's Progress and I want to be with her.

BONNIE: I know what they are thinking but I know he isn't dead. My Dad is pulling pints and serving alcohol to under-sixteens because how else can he keep the business going and I know he does it and I know it's wrong but if you tell I'll report you to Miss Spivak. My Dad didn't pick up because he's on the phone calling my mother names for leaving us and he can't understand why I don't hate her for leaving us. If I were in her shoes I would have done the same.

JANE: Bonnie...

PENNY: Bonnie is not listening. Bonnie is opening the door to The Pilgrim's Progress. I can't look.

JANE: Bonnie, please don't...

ERIC: I want to say...

SAMSON: Please be alive. We need an adult.

BONNIE: I am at the door and I hear a sound from inside.

What did I tell you?

Dad!

ERIC: She pushes against the body blocking the door. I run to help her.

BONNIE: Dad! Dad!

PETER: She's in.

ERIC: And I'm craning my neck over her to see...

Felicity?

PENNY: She looks at us like she has always looked at us, like she doesn't care about anything, not even herself.

BONNIE: Felicity, where's my Dad?

ALBERT: And Felicity whose voice no one has ever heard does not need to say anything.

PETER: She doesn't need to tell Bonnie to look behind the counter.

BONNIE: Dad!

I go behind the counter and he's, he's...

BONNIE falls into ERIC's arms sobbing. The others gather around them in silence.

DENISE: I look to Jane and to Peter.

Someone's got to say it.

We've got to keep moving. We've got to save ourselves before whatever this thing is catches up with us.

GEORGE: Denise!

DENISE: I'm sorry but we've got to keep moving.

PETER: And I'm glad that Denise said it and not me.

JANE: And I'm glad that Denise said it and not me.

PETER: Eric...

ERIC: Leave us.

ALBERT: Eric...

ERIC: Just go.

GEORGE: Eric.

ERIC: Fuck off.

GEORGE: He's forgiven me the way knob heads forgive each other. We're friends again.

Where do we go now?

DENISE: It's clear we're the only survivors.

SAMSON: I sob uncontrollably, but Denise has no time for my tears. Angie takes my hand. She understands.

DENISE: We get out of town. We head for the station. We jump on the next train out of here.

NICHOLAS: No one says what's on my mind.

ANGIE: No one says what's on my mind.

FELICITY: SAMSON: I'm not going home. I don't want to see Mum and Dad looking like Bonnie's Dad…

DENISE: It's up the road. Come on.

The rest look to JANE and PETER.

JANE: …Let's go.

ANGIE: Jane…

She ignores me. She's still angry that I told that she and ERIC were going out when she was still with PETER. Never mind that PETER forgave her. Never mind that ERIC has always wanted BONNIE.

PETER: Jane, with what happened with Bonnie, maybe I should tell them/

JANE: Tell them? No.

PETER: Jane.

JANE: Don't you think I've been humiliated enough for one day?

PETER: If I explain to them about us/

JANE: I said no!

GEORGE: Sh!

NICHOLAS: A noise.

GEORGE: It's coming from the station. There's someone in the station!

ANGIE: We're getting out of here! Now stop crying will you!

DENISE: Hello!

ALBERT: Hello!

BROWN: Denise? Albert?

ALBERT: Mr. Brown?

SAMSON: Mr. Brown!

PENNY: We're all relieved. Someone else has survived.

JANE: An adult has survived.

PETER: Thank you, Father.

CRAIG: Mr. Brown will have the answers. He'll know what's going on. He'll tell them this is not my fault.

BROWN: Bella! Come see who's here.

PETER: Bella...

CRAIG: Oh my God, Bella.

NICHOLAS: Now it will be out in the open, the question that's been on all our minds ever since this thing happened.

BELLA enters. Her head is bandaged.

BELLA: Hi guys.

They rush to hug BELLA, except for CRAIG, out of guilt, and FELICITY, who is being herself.

GEORGE: We cry tears of joy and for the first time since whatever this is we laugh.

JANE: And I'm crying because I'm glad that I'm no longer responsible for these people anymore.

SAMSON: I'm crying because, well I was crying already.

CRAIG: I'm crying and I'm saying I'm sorry and I'm crying and I'm saying I'm sorry...

NICHOLAS: Bella laughs at Craig... She calls him a silly boy and says, and says it was an accident and that it's not his fault?

BELLA: The doctor says my wounds will heal. There'll be no scars. And my hair will grow back.

ANGIE: Mr. Brown says they were at the hospital when it began.

BROWN: We ran out into the street.

BELLA: It was horrible. People were dropping like flies, cars were crashing into each other.

JANE: They tried to drive out of town. The roads are blocked with jack-knifed cars.

BELLA: We came to the station. We've been here for hours.

BROWN: Not one scheduled train has passed by in either direction.

GEORGE: What does it mean?

PENNY: Somebody/

DENISE: Somebody knows something.

PETER: What do we do?

NICHOLAS: Stop pretending like we don't know who's to blame for this.

PETER: What do you mean, Nick?

NICHOLAS: You know what I mean! It's his fault.

CRAIG: I didn't do anything.

NICHOLAS: He made the chemical!

JANE: Nicholas, calm down.

NICHOLAS: He tried to kill me with it! He's killed all my friends, he's killed my parents.

CRAIG: I didn't!

PETER: Nicholas!

ANGIE: I scream as Nick charges at Craig.

PETER: I rush to help Mr. Brown restrain Nicholas, Nicholas whose rage is tearing him apart.

CRAIG: I didn't do it!

NICHOLAS: Murderer!

JANE: And he breaks free from Mr. Brown and Peter, and he runs away towards the shopping centre.

DENISE: Nicholas!

PENNY: George and Albert run after him.

CRAIG: I'm sorry. I'm so, so sorry.

BROWN: It's not your fault, Craig. If anything you're the reason we're alive.

CRAIG: What?

BELLA: Think about it. We're the only ones who breathed in the fumes in chemistry class. We're the only survivors.

PENNY: You mean we're immune to whatever has killed everyone?

BROWN: You saved us Craig. You're a hero.

CRAIG: I was trying to be Scarecrow.

JANE: And I'm so relieved because I was thinking it.

DENISE: And I'm so relieved because I was thinking it.

PETER: And I'm so relieved because I was thinking it.

GEORGE and ALBERT enter.

GEORGE: We lost him.

JANE: Mr. Brown says he cannot leave Nicholas behind. Mr. Brown says he will go after him. But we cannot stay here.

PENNY: Denise who is smarter than all of us says we should go down to the navy base.

DENISE: If anywhere is safe it's there. They'll know what's going on. They'll have an evacuation plan.

PENNY: And I'm wondering why I didn't think of it first.

BROWN: Brilliant idea, Denise. I'll meet you there.

GEORGE: What about Eric and Bonnie?

PETER: We'll check on them on the way.

SAMSON: I'll come with you.

BROWN: Go with the others. I won't be long. Peter, Jane, you're in charge.

PETER: OK.

SAMSON: He gives Jane his number and he's gone. Why didn't he just let Nicholas go? These stupid kids.

JANE: I'm back in charge. I look in their eyes. I'm glad Peter is with me, because he's all that's keeping me from losing it.

PETER: Father, do not desert me. Please, do not desert me.

Her Majesty's Naval Base.

PENNY: Hello!

JANE: It can't be.

DENISE: Hello!

GEORGE: No way.

BELLA: Albert, why is the place deserted?

ALBERT: Why are you asking me?

BELLA: You were here before, to shoot your video.

ALBERT: They must have left afterwards.

DENISE: A whole navy just upped and left?

ALBERT: Yeah.

DENISE: In the middle of a crisis? They must have known what was happening. They couldn't have just left without checking for survivors.

ALBERT: You're the smart one. You figure it out.

JANE: Peter and Angie return from checking out the barracks. And I'm hoping...

PETER: There's no one here.

JANE: Not even a body?

DENISE: They must have known what was going on.

PETER: Albert. When you came here, did you notice them acting strange?

ALBERT: Why is everyone asking me these questions?

JANE: You never came here, did you?

ALBERT: Of course I did.

JANE: Stop lying!

GEORGE: We wasted our time coming here.

PETER: There is no evacuation plan.

DENISE: There is no one to save us.

ALBERT: And I wonder why am I keeping up this lie? No one believes me anyway. So I hide under the uncertain silence.

ANGIE: How the hell do we get out of here?

PETER: Felicity who has wandered off returns. She points back to where she is coming from.

JANE: Why can't you just talk, Felicity? Just say what you want to say.

The frustration is getting to me. The others follow her, even Samson who had broken off from us to sulk. So I go along with them.

Hold it together, Jane.

Where are we going?

FELICITY: JANE: Felicity, I'm talking to you.

FELICITY:

JANE: That's it. I'm not taking another step until you tell us...

PETER: And there it is, right at the farthest corner of the base.

DENISE: A frigate! The HMS Millgarth.

GEORGE: We're saved! We're saved!

On board the frigate, HMS Millgarth.

PENNY: *(On her phone.)* I'm letting Eric and Bonnie know we're here.

SAMSON: I'll call Mr. Brown.

ANGIE: There's no one on board.

GEORGE: But why leave only this ship behind?

PENNY: I can't get a signal.

ALBERT: And Peter says we'd better learn how to pilot the ship, and I can't tell if he's serious or not.

PENNY: Can you get a signal?

SAMSON: No. I can't go online either.

JANE: And everyone's trying their phones.

SAMSON: And I'm worried because how will Mr. Brown know where to find us?

BELLA: How will Eric and Bonnie know we're here?

GEORGE: And the TV in the mess room is using an episode of *Coronation Street* to tease us with normality.

PENNY: The ship must have a radio.

And I don't care that I said it before Denise.

PETER: And I'm asking God, are you punishing me? Have I brought this upon us?

I take a deep breath as we huddle around Denise as she figures out how to work the radio.

DENISE: I look for the on switch but I can't find it and I'm going to press every damn button until this bloody radio comes on.

And it's right in front of me. Calm down, Denise.

I press it.

I feel like I've saved the world.

Everyone cheers with relief as the radio comes on.

DENISE: Hello, is there anybody there?

SAMSON: Hello? Hello!

RADIO 1: Containment of the leak on HMS Millgarth has failed. Given wind speed and direction the gas will spread to the whole country within the week.

ALL: Hello!

Can you hear us!

RADIO 1: The PM has informed the Queen. We've been given the all clear. Over.

ALL: Hello! Hello!

RADIO 1: Commence missile launch in ten minutes. Over.

SAMSON: What?

DENISE: Oh my God.

RADIO 2: Can you confirm there are no survivors? Over.

RADIO 1: Confirmed. The gas has a one hundred per cent fatality rate. Over.

PENNY: We're here! We're here!

RADIO 2: Commencing missile launch in ten minutes. Over and out.

PETER: No.

DENISE: No, no, no...

Hello? Come in, please! Can you hear us!

GEORGE: Through the panic we realize that we are on board the ship responsible for the leak.

PETER: And I'm shouting at everyone to find the room where the leak is coming from and for Denise to keep trying to communicate to the people on the radio.

PENNY: We're running from room to room racing faster than our heartbeats.

ANGIE: Fumes.

Here! It's here.

GEORGE: And we run to the room, the skull and crossbones on the door. And bodies on the floor – the first victims. This is it.

PETER: And without thinking we open the door.

The stage fills with smoke.

PENNY: Clouds of fumes escape.

ANGIE: We are not afraid of the gas. We are immune.

SAMSON: What do we do?

ANGIE: Find the leak!

PETER: And there it is, gaping like a wound.

GEORGE: And we're crashing into each other searching for anything to plug the leak.

PETER: We're pushing anything into the hole.

SAMSON: You're making it bigger!

ANGIE: Shut up!

PETER: Use a cloth!

SAMSON: Here's duct tape!

GEORGE: And we wrap it round and round and round but it won't stop.

PENNY: And then it stops.

PETER: This is not the flood. This is not Sodom and Gomorrah. This is...

ANGIE: Felicity.

PETER: She has moved the hand of a sailor off a button at the control panel. She has stopped the leak.

GEORGE: We laugh and cheer as we race back to the control room. I'm too happy to notice if Felicity was cheering too.

FELICITY:

PENNY: Denise must have found a way to communicate to the navy.

And we're running and laughing.

CRAIG: And we're saying we've saved ourselves.

GEORGE: We're heroes. We've saved the town.

PETER: We've saved the country.

PENNY: And we sing that everything will be ay-OK, just ay-OK.

PETER: Denise! We've stopped the leak. Denise!

PENNY: Her face says it all. She has never looked more certain of her fear.

SAMSON: I'm trying not to cry.

GEORGE: On the radio that refuses to hear us, they are talking coordinates. This town I love is nothing more than a target on a map for someone to aim out.

CRAIG: They are calculating how many missiles it will take to vaporise the chemical gas that they let leak into the air, the gas that they were going to blame me for leaking.

SAMSON: And I start crying.

PENNY: And I'm saying we saved the country. How can they do this to us?

JANE: And I'm wondering if Britain will miss me the way I miss my parents.

GEORGE: And I'm asking myself if I die will people only remember me for being a knob head.

JANE: Felicity switches off the radio. She is like an angel of death, and I'm too distressed to say that I'm in charge, and that's my job and, and, and...

ANGIE: And I'm asking myself who am I going to tell this to? If there's life on the other side and they ask me to tell all I'll say I'm not that kind of person, not anymore.

PENNY: And I'm saying Denise, you're smart, get us out of here.

DENISE: And I'm thinking, for all my smartness I'm going to die like everyone else.

ALBERT: And I'm saying the gas that made us immune from the gas leak will save us from the bombs. Either I'm lying to myself or I really am that stupid.

SAMSON: And I'm hoping Mr. Brown will turn up. He'll know what to do.

CRAIG: And I'm so relieved I'm not the bad guy.

ANGIE: And I look at my video and I'm thinking to myself, no way am I going to be remembered for this. I delete it and go up to the deck.

SAMSON clocks ANGIE going on deck.

PETER: I'm wondering if God is punishing me and I'm saying to myself, no. God is love, and God made me like this and it is people who think being gay is unnatural. It is people who made this unnatural gas who think they can force you to choose who you love, who force you to hide inside your skin. I know it's not God. And I know he will receive me.

And I know this is not the end times. So I go down on my knees and pray to Him.

GEORGE: And I'm in the mess room looking at the TV flicking the channels. And the news is all about the red carpet at the BAFTAs, and I take a hammer to the TV.

ANGIE: I'm on deck, facing the sea. This looks perfect. *(Holds her phone up to her face. Takes a moment to compose herself. Records.)* Hello. I'm Angie…

SAMSON: And my hand goes after Angie's hand to hold. But like everyone else she is crying in her own way. And I see something, like a ship, or an island and it's moving then it's not moving but it looks like safety to me. And my legs take me over the ship.

ANGIE: *(Holds out her arms.)* Samson!

PETER: And Angie's scream jolts us, and suddenly we're running to the deck and she's pointing out to sea.

PENNY: It's dark. I'm thinking have they come for us?

ALBERT: And I can't see anything.

JANE: And Angie again shouts…

ANGIE: Samson!

JANE: And now we're all screaming out Samson's name, and I don't know why because what's the point and I'm sorry for thinking one less person to worry about.

SAMSON: I can hear them cheering me on, and I'm getting tired but I'm getting closer and it's an island not a ship but there'll be somewhere I can hide and I'll be safe.

PENNY: I can't look. I'm screaming but I can't look.

DENISE: And I know the answer to the question but I won't say it. Not this time.

SAMSON: I can't hear them anymore. My legs stop moving but I can see the island, I can see safety.

They stop shouting. They are hugging each other:

PETER and JANE.

PENNY, DENISE and ALBERT.

GEORGE puts down ANGIE's arms and hugs her.

CRAIG stands alone. FELICITY goes to him and holds his hand. CRAIG hugs her tightly.

PETER: I have this urge to tell everyone that Jane was pretending to be my girlfriend until I was ready to come out and that there was really nothing between us. I had to come out to God first. Jane wouldn't let me. She wouldn't let me think I brought this upon us. But I don't think it matters anymore. And I don't know when it happened but we are holding onto each other. That's what people do when they need each other. They forget the things that don't matter. They just reach out for each other. And if anyone is bothered to think we've made up, we're back together again, fine by me.

JANE: And I'm wondering if Peter is thinking this is his fault, this is Sodom and Gomorrah and Noah and the flood all over again... And I know he's passed that point of guilt, I know because we've been there for each other, so I just worry about myself because it isn't selfish to think of oneself in a situation like this. I just want to think of myself and the things I'll miss and the things I won't get to do and the lives I was going to change.

DENISE: Friday.

GEORGE: What?

DENISE: Friday would have been the bomb.

PETER: And I'm thinking what an insensitive joke to make, and then Jane starts to laugh. And then Albert, and then Angie and then Craig.

CRAIG: And we're all laughing, like Denise had just told the killing joke that cracked Batman's face into a smile.

ALBERT: It's the first cold day of the warmest year since records began.

JANE: *(To PETER.)* I feel so warm.

The lights go very bright. They all look up.

Darkness.

A video phone goes on. We see FELICITY coming into focus.

FELICITY: I don't know what to say. I guess I'd better talk about myself, which is hard because I hate talking. People are always saying stuff they never mean and then they say they take it back after they've said it as if that's possible. My Mum told me Bonnie's Dad is my Dad, and I went see him to ask for myself but he said no he wasn't. I look like my Mum so I'd no way of knowing it but I couldn't tell Bonnie because if I'm her half-sister then I'm the reason why her Mum left. And I don't know if this is of any interest to anyone except Bonnie. But that's all I have to say. So if you get this message, I don't know, make of it whatever. I suppose I should leave a message to the world. Um, yeah. Whatever you do/

The video ends abruptly.

The End.